The Railway Siding

A Play in One Act

Jonathan Holloway

A SAMUEL FRENCH ACTING EDITION

Copyright © 2012 by Jonathan Holloway
All Rights Reserved
THE RAILWAY SIDING is fully protected under the copyright laws of the United States of America, the British Commonwealth, including Canada, and all other countries of the Copyright Union. All rights, including professional and amateur stage productions, recitation, lecturing, public reading, motion picture, radio broadcasting, television and the rights of translation into foreign languages are strictly reserved.

ISBN 978-0-573-12229-3

www.SamuelFrench.com
www.SamuelFrench-London.co.uk

FOR PRODUCTION ENQUIRIES

UNITED STATES AND CANADA
Info@SamuelFrench.com
1-866-598-8449

UNITED KINGDOM AND EUROPE
Theatre@SamuelFrench-London.co.uk
020-7255-4302

Each title is subject to availability from Samuel French, depending upon country of performance. Please be aware that *THE RAILWAY SIDING* may not be licensed by Samuel French in your territory. Professional and amateur producers should contact the nearest Samuel French office or licensing partner to verify availability.

CAUTION: Professional and amateur producers are hereby warned that *THE RAILWAY SIDING* is subject to a licensing fee. Publication of this play(s) does not imply availability for performance. Both amateurs and professionals considering a production are strongly advised to apply to Samuel French before starting rehearsals, advertising, or booking a theatre. A licensing fee must be paid whether the title(s) is presented for charity or gain and whether or not admission is charged. Professional/Stock licensing fees are quoted upon application to Samuel French.

No one shall make any changes in this title(s) for the purpose of production. No part of this book may be reproduced, stored in a retrieval system, or transmitted in any form, by any means, now known or yet to be invented, including mechanical, electronic, photocopying, recording, videotaping, or otherwise, without the prior written permission of the publisher. No one shall upload this title(s), or part of this title(s), to any social media websites.

For all enquiries regarding motion picture, television, and other media rights, please contact Samuel French.

THE RAILWAY SIDING

The original radio version of *The Railway Siding* was comissioned by the BBC and broadcast on Radio 4 as its Afternoon Drama on Thursday 12th November 2009.

This stage version was first performed on 26th September 2012 at the Questors Theatre, West London, with the following cast:

Tom
The Stationmaster } Robert Vass
London Rail Steward
Jack Webb   Gareth Jones
The Train Guard   Simon Higginson
Mrs Hope Cairns   Victoria Pringle

Directed by Sarah Stoddart
Designed by Sarah Stoddart
Lighting design by Richard Mead
Sound design by Paul Wilson

CHARACTERS

Tom, Jack's London architect friend, RP, world weary, lounge suit
Jack Webb, late 40s, educated estuarine, unshaven, Levis, heavy, expensive, unpolished brogues, an expensive but now shapeless hand-knitted chunky jumper
The Stationmaster, Welsh, old British Rail-style overcoat and peaked cap
The Train Guard, 50s, Gloucestershire, old-fashioned British Rail-style uniform
Mrs Hope Cairns, clipped RP, dressed exactly like Celia Johnson in *Brief Encounter*
London Rail Steward, Welsh, modern garish rail uniform

N.B. Tom, The Stationmaster and the London Rail Steward can be played by the same actor.

Time — the present/1948

Other plays by Jonathan Holloway
published by Samuel French Ltd:

The Dark
Darkness Falls
Les Misérables (adapted from the novel by Victor Hugo)
The Monkey's Paw
Nicholas Nickleby

THE RAILWAY SIDING

Scene 1

A dining alcove in a seaside cottage

There are two rows of bench seats with a table between them UC. *These do not need literally to be reproductions of a railway carriage, but ought to be able to give that impression. They hint at multiple locations, including a dining alcove in a seaside cottage. Upstage of this arrangement there is a window suspended in darkness. Again, it does not need to be a reproduction of a carriage window, although it will be used to give that impression. This window should be "frosted" so that it can take various lighting effects. There is a pile of expensive architectural journals and coffee table art books tumbled about* DR. *There is an elegant "designer" coffee table* DL *on which sits a trendy Mexican beer tray with a half empty bottle of Wild Turkey American bourbon whiskey, a chunky glass tumbler, three American-style diner coffee mugs, a nearly empty cafetière, a Claris Cliff teapot, a matching milk jug and an open packet of malted biscuits. There is a trendy Art Nouveau-style phone with a practical circular dialler. The few items we can see all suggest art-house style — mostly bought from places like Heals. Argos is unknown in this environment. Next to the coffee table* L *there's an upright Bauhaus-style armchair — a chromium frame with black leather support for the sitter.* R *of the coffee table and almost* C *there's a Victorian piano stool. Amongst the debris* DR *there's a heavy, old, expensive tweed jacket, a large fashionable canvas satchel and an artist's portfolio that has seen better days*

It's dark on stage. As the house lights dim to black-out, play in the Godley and Creme track, "Under Your Thumb"

Jack takes up his position and the Lights come up to reveal a semi-darkened stage with pools of "downlighter" light illuminating the coffee table area DL *and the surface of the table* UC. *There is a projected image of the moon as later described in the text visible in the* R *corner of the window frame. Tom is standing behind the coffee table holding the phone in his left hand and the receiver to his ear with the right hand. He has his back to the audience and is upstage of the coffee table, half in darkness*

The music fades to reveal the sound of surf on a long West Wales beach off in the distance. A vertical downlighter comes up R *and Tom walks into the light*

Tom Are you still there, Jack?
Jack Yes, of course.
Tom You're not drunk, are you?
Jack No. Just tired. And I think I'm coming down with something.
Tom I don't really like you being stuck down there on your own so far from civilization.
Jack There's a Londis in the village. And I've got a telly! Tim Wonnacott and I usually get together bargain hunting around lunchtime.
Tom I've gone out on a limb for you, Jack.
Jack I know, Tom.
Tom I need the drawings by next Monday.
Jack Received and understood.
Tom And they'd better be as good as you said they'd be, otherwise we're finished. No more favours. Understood?
Jack Absolutely.
Tom Have you spoken to Harriet?
Jack No.
Tom Don't you think you ought to?

Scene 1 3

Jack No, Tom. I'm totally focused on your drawings right now, and I don't want to fry my brain with another hour of recriminations.

Tom All right, Jack. Call me at the weekend. Put me out of my misery, will you?

The R downlighter fades

Tom exits R

Jack replaces the receiver on the cradle of the phone he's still holding and sighs. He turns to downstage and puts the phone on the coffee table. He picks up the tumbler and examines it, looking for traces of previous contents. He cleans the inside of the tumbler with the cuff of his shirt and then dashes some whiskey into it. While leaning over to do this, he seems to sense the audience and looks up to focus on us, then stands upright surveying the auditorium and after a fortifying slug of whiskey begins to address us. During the following speech he ranges about the room

Jack There are many uncertainties in life. But as sure as eggs is eggs, no one was going to write about me in the Architectural Review ever again. No. (*He sighs*) The recession made me redundant, and after the partners let me go I did pick up a bit of work, but the phone calls got fewer, and I got phobic about going into town to discuss jobs I knew I wouldn't get. One day I was walking back from taking Dot to school and I realized my feet were each making a different sound. And I looked down, and saw I had odd shoes on. Falling apart, you see. And — cliché upon cliché — I was taking altogether too much interest in our Slovenian girl, Matilde — who we didn't really need anymore. No, all in all, there wasn't much joy in the household. I got boring, like men do. Whining, ogling, drinking at lunchtime and snoozing the afternoon away until I had to get Dot from school — for which I was usually late.

Then, out of the blue I got a shot at something marvellous. You see in here, I'm not an unshaven old lag. In here I'm actually enthusiastic about building things. I only needed a bit of luck to bring that out again. Tom, the only one of my university mates who's kept in touch, phoned me. His practice had become very chi-chi and was bucking the trend, and actually doing really well. He remembered I'd droned on years ago about ways of incorporating innovative use of wood into new builds. Ironically, all I was doing now was knocking together aluminium box section extensions for the well-heeled of Wimbledon Willage. But anyway, Tom was in discussion about a new health centre that needed to make a visual statement, and integrating oak into the design was a stipulation of the funders. It also had to be cantilevered so it could hang out and over the main line out of St Pancras. Before I knew it, he'd subbed the job to me. (*He sighs*) But then, of course, I had to get on and actually do it. And given I wasn't what the Americans would call "in a good place", this turned into something of a problem. Then, bang! Harriet suggested I should leave home for a while. (*Pause*) I think she might even have been having an affair. (*Pause*) I can't be sure, but there were just too many loose ends. (*Pause*) Anyway. I went to her parents' holiday place in West Wales. (*He indicates the room he's standing in*) Right on a cliff. Beautiful. Solitude. Peace. And of course, weak fool that I am, within thirty-four hours I'd got an aerial installed and was wasting my time on daytime TV and sniffing around a woman I met who's a teacher at the local primary school. All right! I know I'm coming across as a bit seedy. But — and it's a big BUT — that isn't the point. I'm a human being, and a human being needs some source of pride. Some reason why he thinks he deserves a slot in existence. To know someone, somewhere, actually admires him.

Over a period of several minutes, the image of the moon in the window describes an arc from top left to top right of the frame. This can be achieved simply by cross-fading from one image to the next in a subtly "stylized" fashion

Scene 2

So, let's not be so hard on ourselves — on me. Anyway, there is light at the end of all this, because suddenly I sort of woke up! Literally and figuratively. I'd spent half the night lying awake as the moon described her arc across the skylight above me, and by the time it was light the whole idea was formed in my head. (*He goes to the benches* UC *and sits at the table as if accompanying the memory of his night of feverish work with gestures that repeat drawing up plans*) I lighted on the idea of big sweeping composite arches — oak and stainless steel, like the laminate in a long bow — from which the cabin structure would hang. I didn't have a Mac with me. Just rotring, paper and portfolio. With forty-eight hours to go I worked up a set of pretty impressive drawings. I couldn't believe it. I was enjoying myself — actually enjoying myself — and I felt really good about what I'd done. But ... But ... But, I didn't finish until ten o'clock at night. (*He suddenly lunges for the articles* DR, *dressing in the heavy jacket, sorting items and stuffing them into his satchel, zipping up the portfolio, and then stands staring at us like a breathless child ready for school*) And those drawings were due to be on Tom's desk at ten the next morning. My only chance was the overnight train to London. I got a cab from the house to Haverfordwest, and waited for the quarter-to-twelve train. There I was with my stuff. With half an hour to spare. The only person on the platform. The rain tapping gently, evenly on the station roof.

SCENE 2

The station platform

Cross-fade to interim blue wash to allow the actors to get into position. The scene change is accompanied by a subtle excerpt from "Under Your Thumb"

Jack stands C

The Stationmaster steps on from R and stands staring directly at him

Both hunch against the weather

Cross-fade to the night-time platform illuminated by a powerful yellow "sodium" key light from R. The music fades away to steady heavy rain

Stationmaster Good-evening, sir.
Jack (*jumping*) Heavens!
Stationmaster Sorry. I didn't mean to frighten you.
Jack I didn't see you.
Stationmaster Not long now, then you'll be out of the weather.
Jack Is the London train on time?
Stationmaster Yes. Just another five minutes.
Jack It's early, then?
Stationmaster No. Right on time.

Jack leans out off the front of the stage, looking to right and left as if searching for a train, and we realize the front of the stage has become the edge of the platform. Of course, as soon as he leans out, he gets rained on

Jack I must have got it wrong. I thought the London train was at eleven forty-five. Good job I got here early. This next one — it isn't some slow train that goes to London via Carlisle or something, is it? I'm just wondering if I ought to wait for the eleven forty-five after all? Be on the safe side. I'm on a mission, you see?
Stationmaster No need for that. This is what they used to call the milk train. It goes straight through, so you won't be interfered with by drunks getting on at Swansea.
Jack Oh, well that's all right, then.
Stationmaster If you were my family, I wouldn't want you getting a punch in the gob. I knew a fellow whose brother-in-

Scene 2

law was killed with a hammer up in Liverpool by some bloke who wanted the Christmas presents he was carrying. It's a sad world. You have to do something. We have to use our discretion. Stand our ground against casual cruelty, as you might say.

Jack Er ... yes, I suppose we do.

Stationmaster Of course it's not like the old days when a stationmaster was a proper job with responsibilities and authority. But some of us still like to try to do the right thing — if you understand me. I planted the flowers myself, you know.

Jack What flowers?

Stationmaster On the other platform. It was my idea to use old tyres to make the planters. I painted them white, you know? Just to look at them, you wouldn't have guessed what they really were. We learnt to re-use, didn't we? Keep things as civilized as you can, no matter what they throw at us. Mind you. This time next year I won't be here. I love the railway, but it's not the same and I've got my retirement coming up. (*Pause*) London, then?

Jack That's right.

Stationmaster Next train on this platform.

Jack Thank you.

Stationmaster I'm off to pack up my things. As soon as your train leaves I'll be locking up. 'Night. (*He starts to walk away*)

There is the rumble of the train coming into the station, the diesel locomotive thrumming and the air brakes squealing

Jack "spots" the train as if it is drawing up across the front of the stage

Jack Good-night.

Stationmaster You'll be all right.

Jack Old rolling stock, by the look of it.

Stationmaster (*calling to him*) That's right. Well, it's the middle of the night, after all. (*Suddenly official*) London! Direct train to London, Paddington.

The Stationmaster blows his whistle. Jack spins towards the chair by the coffee table

The Stationmaster exits

Cross-fade to blue wash as Jack unloads his bags and collapses into the armchair

"Under Your Thumb" plays

Scene 3

On board the train

The Guard arrives and stands over Jack, positioned UR *of him*

The Lights come up on a cosy dappled pattern of ad-hoc illumination provided by inadequate old style bulbs. The image projected on the window changes to that of a moon with vaporous clouds drifting across it — a night for mysterious things!

"Under Your Thumb" gives way to the continuous grinding noise as the train travels along seamless modern rail tracks

Realizing the Guard is looming over him, Jack feverishly searches baggage and pockets for his ticket

Guard Good-evening, sir.
Jack Oh!
Guard Sorry to disturb you. Can I see your ticket, please?
Jack Yes, of course. (*Struggling to find it*) I'm very sorry.
Guard Best that I wake you up now, then you can settle down properly.
Jack I never sleep on trains usually.
Guard Well, you were starting to doze off just now. You're all right, are you, sir?

Scene 3   9

Jack Yes. Why?
Guard Not ill?
Jack No.
Guard (*taking and clipping the ticket*) Thank you.
Jack Oh, clippers.
Guard Yes, sir.
Jack Only now it's usually an indecipherable biro scrawl. Like a doctor's prescription.
Guard (*regarding Jack with a wry expression*) You look a little feverish.
Jack I could do with a hot drink.
Guard We don't have a catering carriage, I'm afraid.
Jack (*yawning*) No, I wasn't expecting one.
Guard Seven hours fifty-seven minutes. It's a long time. But I've put the urn on, and when you're ready you can knock on the pass door at the back of the train. I'll be happy to give you a brew.
Jack That's very kind.

Jack doesn't notice that the sound of the continuous track has cross-faded to the "clackety-clack" of an old-fashioned segmented line

Guard It's no trouble to be helpful. People travelling at this time usually have something going on, and why shouldn't I make their lives a bit easier?
Jack "Going on?" (*Pause*) Thank you. Is it just me tonight?
Guard Not sure.
Jack Well, you don't stop again, do you? (*Pause*) Something's different.
Guard Sorry?
Jack The ... er ... the noise. It's like the old segmented track. We're continuous now, aren't we?
Guard Yes. That's right. But this train uses some older sections of the line.
Jack Really? Ha! You learn something new every day, don't you?

Guard Indeed. Or even every night. Or at least, you try to. We might stop, if there's a need. For a little wait in the sidings after Swindon. But as far as I know, yes, it's just you.

Jack And you, too.

Guard Yes, of course.

Jack And the driver.

Guard Of course. Yes. There has to be a driver. I like to keep the passengers close by when there's only a few.

Jack Or just one.

Guard Indeed. Feels cosier like that. (*Pause*) Mind if I sit down for a moment? (*He sits on the piano stool*)

Jack Not at all.

Guard (*sighing as he sits*) It's been a long night.

Jack Has it?

Guard It's always night for me. I only work nights. Day is night, as you might say. I prefer it like that. Well, I should say, I preferred it like that. But recently I've started to change my mind. Too much that's new. On board used to be a world apart. But it's less so, now.

Jack Oh, yes?

Guard I love the railways. My working life has been a childhood dream come true. Not many can say that, can they?

Jack I suppose not.

Guard And I like these late trains. Because —

Jack Because what?

Guard Because sometimes you see ... unusual sights.

Jack What sights?

Guard All kinds of things. I see what one might call stories, I suppose. Or bits from the middle of stories. You don't know where they came from or where they'll end.

Jack Yes. I know what you mean. Like the other day. We passed some green back gardens and there was this man bouncing on a child's trampoline. His arms tight to his sides, looking straight ahead. Up and down. Very odd.

Guard On platforms, sometimes I think I see ghosts of people. Chattering away. Or just standing watching the trains go by. Sometimes, the shadow of a wish ...

Scene 3

Jack Pardon?
Guard Oh, I didn't mean, literally.
Jack I see.
Guard I read a lot. I have always had a lively imagination. My parents worried about that.
Jack It doesn't sound like something to worry about.
Guard My mum was a bit bonkers, and her sister was in a home all her life. No, a lively imagination wasn't wanted where I grew up.
Jack That's a bit sad.
Guard As a little 'un I even liked to think about the conversations, the cries, the tender moments — all the things that might happen on a train. I was often put with the lady next door. When my mum wasn't so well. And her boys had an "O" gauge clockwork railway. Fantastic, it was. And I used to sit over it like God looking down, watching it go round, thinking about the people inside.
Jack Do you write any of this down?
Guard I prefer reading. I tried to write it down, but it wasn't very good. There weren't any surprises. You read for the surprises, don't you? No point in reading what you writ yourself. Best left to the professionals, I think.
Jack I've never really fallen for trains, myself.
Guard Well, loving the railways, now ... it's an easy thing to know and a hard thing to explain. There are lots of ... I don't know ... lots of "sides" to it. You're on rails, which are peculiar things when you think about them. You can't ride bicycles on them, you can't drive lorries on them and you can't really even walk on them. They have only one purpose — to carry a box full of human souls from one place to another. Once you're on a train and it's moving ... well, you can't just stop when you fancy, can you? It's not like driving a car. You're stuck, and there's nothing you can do about it, and you're in a different world. A different kind of life. Speeding to somewhere else ... I don't know ... perhaps you could become someone else.
Jack Do you think that's possible?

Guard Do you want to be someone else?
Jack Oh, most definitely. Don't you?
Guard Perhaps I did. Once. But that's all over with. I'm fixed now. This is me forever.
Jack That's sad too.
Guard Nonsense. Once I knew. That made everything easier. It was a relief.
Jack It would be wonderful to get off this train and be new ... different ... better.
Guard Anything's possible. Now, the old steam trains — they really had it. Whistles blowing. Screeching through the night. As I say — heading towards something else, and you don't yet know what it is. Filled up with people loving, longing. I'd better get on. (*He hauls himself out of the seat*) Don't be shy about knocking on the door if you fancy a cuppa.
Jack Thanks.

Jack leans his head back as if sliding into a doze

We cross-fade to "Under Your Thumb" with the lighting change

The Lights cross-fade to blue "scene-change" state

Scene 4

The same

A Woman, Hope Cairns, enters slowly, walking as if distracted, and slides into the R window seat, then slowly turns her head to look out of the window. The music plays on and nothing happens for a full thirty seconds. Jack is suddenly awake and worried he may have lost something, and so gets up to pat his pockets, then searches the ground behind the chair

Scene 4

The Lights come up, restoring the carriage state

The sound cross-fades back to the clickety-clack of the tracks to which has been added the laborious chuffing of a steam engine labouring up a long gradient

Having recovered his ticket from the floor, Jack finds himself L *of the booth seats, staring at the seated Woman*

Jack Hello.
Woman Pardon?
Jack Sorry. I didn't mean to frighten you.
Woman Oh, don't worry about that. Can't be helped. Everything frightens me these days.
Jack I was dozing, then I woke up and saw there was someone else. You must have got on before me, at Fishguard? I hope you don't mind being bothered. I woke up and felt very cold.
Woman I don't think it's cold.
Jack Not now. No. But sometimes when you snooze, you get cold, don't you? Something to do with one's metabolism.
Woman I don't really know what you mean.
Jack I shouldn't be bothering you. Perhaps I was having a dream. But I woke up feeling really awful.
Woman You don't look very well.
Jack Would you rather I left you alone?
Woman I suppose that depends.
Jack Yes. Perhaps I shouldn't have come over. You look upset.
Woman I spend too much time alone.
Jack When did you get on?

Silence

Listen, the guard said he'd make me a hot drink, as there are so few passengers. I wonder, would you like one too?
Woman That's very nice of him. I've never heard of such a thing.

Jack Well, there's no buffet carriage.
Woman No.
Jack So, tea or coffee?
Woman They have them in America, I believe.
Jack What?
Woman Buffet carriages. Only they call them cars, I think.
Jack Do they?
Woman Yes. They call them cars not carriages. One sees them on the films. Those Americans, eh?
Jack They have them on this line too, if you're sane enough to travel at a sensible hour.
Woman Do they? Really? Tea, please. The coffee tastes so awful these days.
Jack Earl Grey?
Woman Pardon?
Jack Ordinary?
Woman Ordinary will do. Thank you.

Cross-fade to the now familiar "scene change" blue

The sound cross-fades to "Under Your Thumb"

The Woman turns her face to the window

Scene 5

The Guard's compartment

The Guard enters and sits on the piano stool. Jack walks downstage to stand just UL *of the Guard*

Cross-fade to the clickety-clack of the rails and the steady chuffing of the steam engine. The Lights change to the enclosed environment of the Guard's compartment — just the coffee table downlighter

Scene 5 15

The Guard is studying an ancient bound railway timetable as if it were a photo album. He is pleased to renew acquaintance with some now disused lines and services

Guard Hello, can I help you?
Jack You said to knock if we wanted a drink?
Guard So I did. Tea? Coffee?
Jack Coffee for me. Tea for the lady.
Guard Coming up. (*Pause*) What lady?
Jack The woman sitting near me.
Guard There's a woman sitting next to you?
Jack Yes. You didn't look at her ticket.
Guard I didn't see her.
Jack I went off to sleep again.
Guard Ah yes, the gentleman who claims "never to sleep on trains".
Jack That's right. Anyway, I have been. So, when I woke up I noticed the top of her head a few rows away.
Guard Does she look like I ought to see her ticket?
Jack No. Not particularly.
Guard I'll leave her to it, then.
Jack Why does it take nearly eight hours to do the trip?
Guard We allow that long because sometimes we have to go into a siding. (*Pause*) So the freight trains can get past us.
Jack Will that be happening tonight?
Guard Yes. I wasn't sure before, but I've just had news we will be stopping. They'll put us in a siding near Swindon for an hour, or so.
Jack For the freight trains?
Guard Yes, for the sake of the freight trains.
Jack (*after a pause*) I say! Listen.
Guard Listen to what?
Jack The engine. It sounds like a steam train.
Guard Does it? (*He pauses to listen*) I suppose it does, a bit. But what you're hearing is the sound of the telegraph poles whooshing past.

Jack Really?

Guard Yes. Those and the tunnels. They play all kinds of tricks.

Jack Oh, mugs! It's always plastic cups these days.

Guard I saved these when they changed everything. I've actually got quite a collection. All with the names of the various private companies from the past printed on them. Pre-British Rail. I'm happier in the past. Biscuit?

Jack (*struggling with the idea of carrying cups and biscuits*) Yes, that would be nice. But ... erm ...

Guard I'll tuck them in your top pocket, shall I?

Jack I haven't got ... I didn't think I had a top pocket. Oh, heavens.

Guard What's the matter?

Jack I've put the wrong jacket on. I was in such a state trying to leave the house. The other day I went out with odd shoes on too. I didn't notice until I realized my footsteps sounded wrong. This must have belonged to my wife's grandfather.

Guard Comes to us all. Mind you, it's a quality garment. Rather stylish. They don't make 'em like that now.

Jack Well, they do, but only if you're rich.

Guard It fits you well. Could have been made for you.

Jack Yes, I think I might hang on to it.

Guard Here are your biscuits.

Jack Thanks.

Guard Don't be afraid to come back later. I shan't be sleeping. I don't like to miss the journey.

Jack Right — oh.

Very short cross-fade to blue — just enough time to allow the Guard to slip off the stage towards L

   Guard exits

Sound effect: we remain in the world of steam railways

Scene 6   17

Jack turns on the spot to face the Woman UR *of him and proffers the cups as evidence of success*

SCENE 6

The railway carriage

Cross-fade to the carriage state

Jack Your tea. (*Putting down the mugs*) And a biscuit. Never seen those before. But they look OK.
Woman Thank you.
Jack Shall I go back to my seat, or would you like company?
Woman Oh, no. Do stay. If you want to.
Jack (*sitting down opposite her — then, after a pause*) Please, you'll have to forgive me, but have I met you somewhere before?
Woman No. I don't think so. That's a nice jacket.
Jack It whiffs a bit, actually.
Woman I hadn't noticed.
Jack BO and tobacco. You look nice.
Woman I think I'm a bit of a fright.
Jack No, really. You look great. I suppose you're in fashion, or something like that?
Woman No. Not at all.
Jack It's just the way you look ... the way you dress and do your hair, and so on.
Woman I think I'm rather plain. We don't have ... you know ... spare money for things like fashion. Besides, I don't go anywhere.
Jack I had a girlfriend who wore her hair like you. And she had those shoulders, too. It's come back again, hasn't it? New Burlesque, and all that. (*Pause*) Am I talking rubbish?
Woman The way you speak is a little confusing.
Jack When we were students, we all used to dress like that. We smoked Black Cats and Capstan Full Strengths and hung

out in an art deco café near Bethnal Green ... oh, God — what was it called?
Woman I'm afraid I wouldn't know. I've never been to Bethnal Green. You shouldn't swear.
Jack Sorry, I didn't realize I had. (*Pause*) You haven't touched your tea. Or your biscuit.
Woman I haven't spoken to anyone in a long while. I'm having trouble keeping up.
Jack Where are you from?
Woman East Grinstead.
Jack And you're going back there now, are you?
Woman I'm trying to.
Jack Do you mind me asking what you're doing so far from home?
Woman It's a long story. (*Pause*) No, actually, I don't know why I said that. It's quite a short story. Short and stupid.
Jack Oh my, you look so very sad. (*Silence*) Do you have children?

She bursts into tears

I'm sorry. I was only making conversation. Please don't cry. Are you all right?
Woman No, actually. I'm not at all, all right.
Jack I see. (*Pause*) I wasn't spinning you a line. I am absolutely sure I know you. What do you do?
Woman I have children.
Jack And a partner?
Woman What sort of partner?
Jack Do you live with someone?
Woman Of course. My husband.
Jack Oh, I see. Sorry.
Woman I'm such a stupid person. There's so much I don't understand.

The train has been losing momentum for a while

Scene 6

Jack We're definitely slowing down.
Woman Are we? I'd rather we didn't.
Jack The Guard said we'd be stuck outside Swindon for a while.

The train now stops with a slight jolt and everything falls silent

Woman What a fate, eh?
Jack Stuck outside Swindon for a while?
Woman Stuck outside Swindon forever.
Jack I believe they've been particularly badly hit.
Woman Poor things.
Jack Yes. I'm not sure, but I think Honda have shut down almost completely.
Woman Honda? I don't know what that means.
Jack The car plant.
Woman Really, that was hit?
Jack Yes. Very hard. But I think it's looking up. They've started work on the new Jazz.
Woman I don't know anything about jazz. I like jolly things, though.
Jack But I don't believe there are enough jobs for everyone.
Woman People haven't got the money for gramophone records.
Jack (*obviously nonplussed*) No. Certainly not. Anyway, I wouldn't worry, we'll be moving soon enough. The guard said we'd only be here for about an hour. That's funny. It's got very foggy outside. I didn't notice it getting misty, did you? I can't see anything of the shunting yard. We're marooned, by the look of it. (*Pause*) Did you say you have children?
Woman (*after a pause*) Yes. Two lovely children. And a lovely home. It's all so stupid really. I don't know what I was thinking of.
Jack What do you mean?
Woman I was going to meet someone. At Milford Junction.
Jack I'm sorry. I don't know where that is.

Woman I was supposed to get off there, but I didn't. I sat still and went all the way to Fishguard. I've never been there before. There isn't much to speak of about the place, is there?
Jack It's pretty, in a bleak sort of way. A bit like you, actually.
Woman I'm not sure that's a very nice thing to say.
Jack What — "pretty" or "bleak"?
Woman I'm sorry?
Jack I was just making a joke. Misfired. But actually, you are very pretty.
Woman I have a devoted husband who leaves at half-past seven in the morning, and returns at half-past six in the evening. Monday to Friday. And on Saturdays he repairs bits of the house and changes his books at the library, and buys shellfish for tea at the stall by the pub in town. He has started doing fretwork, and he's making my mother a wooden fire screen for Christmas.
Jack Who were you going to meet?
Woman I don't suppose it matters. I'll never see you again. (*Pause*) I was going to meet Jack, with whom I have fallen in love.
Jack I'm guessing that isn't the same man you're married to. So ... falling in love ... wasn't a good thing?
Woman No. But I think perhaps I needed to.
Jack Why?
Woman Because one can't live without love, can one? Not being loved is such a terrible, terrible thing. And it doesn't matter if it has been deliberately taken away, or just fallen silent out of neglect — there's still a dreadful darkness in one that cries out to be illuminated. My husband is a kind man, but I don't believe he loves me.
Jack Have you asked him?
Woman Of course not.
Jack And how did you meet this other ... chap? It is a "chap", I assume.
Woman I wish I could understand what you mean.
Jack It's just, one never knows these days.

Scene 6

Woman It was so silly. We met in a railway café. A chance encounter much like this one. We met six weeks ago and were both captivated. Immediately. We have been seeing each other regularly since. There is nothing ... you know. We touched our fingertips on the table. Those touches were like electric shocks. He is also —

Jack Happily married ... I'm sorry. I wasn't making fun.

Woman You can make fun as much as you like. After all, it is funny, isn't it? Ridiculous that someone like me should expect happiness. After all, I'm not a real person any more. Why couldn't I get used to it? I'm a mother and a wife. "Your mother." "Your wife."

Jack Hey, hey. Calm down. Do you want me to come and sit beside you?

Woman Yes ... No ... (*Pause*) And he has children. And you see we resolved — deliberately, ruthlessly — to abandon our families and run away together. Everything is over and past, and part of our yesterdays. I sat on the train and stared straight ahead, daring him to find me. But he didn't. He wasn't there ... at Milford. I love my husband still, I think. But we all change, and he changed. And he was always cross with me, and didn't take care to be gentle any more. And I think that's why I crumpled when someone new showed me kindness. Showed me I was worthwhile — worth loving.

Jack So you mean, your husband drove you to it?

Woman No he didn't drive me to anything. The absence of love made me do a stupid thing. (*Pause*) Now you're looking sad. I didn't mean to do that to you.

Jack I think perhaps the same thing has happened to my own wife.

Woman But you're kind.

Jack To you, and to other women I meet. And to small animals and children. But at home I don't bother. I've given up trying.

Woman You mustn't do that.

Jack It's too late, I think.

Woman No. I was going back to my husband. It's not too late for you either ...

Jack Jack.
Woman Jack. It's never too late.
Jack I don't know your name.
Woman Probably best. (*She sniffs back a tear*) Oh, dear. Look at us. We shouldn't be talking like this.
Jack The guard was saying train travel changes lives.
Woman It has changed mine.
Jack Will you be able to go home and pick up the threads all right?
Woman I like to think so.
Jack Do you want another cup of tea? That one's gone cold.
Woman Yes, please. Thank you for being so patient.
Jack No. I invited myself into your evening. You are entitled to talk. Are you feeling any better?
Woman I don't know. I think so.
Jack I'll go and fetch some more tea. (*Getting out of his seat*) Don't go anywhere, will you?

There is the sudden lurching sound of the carriages being coupled to a different engine

Cross-fade to the blue wash

Jack walks towards L *and pauses facing off with the mugs in his hands. The Woman looks out at the moon, then at her watch and stands with a sense that she has a task to perform*

> *She eases out of the bench seat, stands, glances over her shoulder at Jack, then walks resolutely off* R

Scene 7

The Guard's compartment

The Lights cross-fade to the L *downlight, leaving the seat vacated by the Woman still warmed*

Scene 8

The Guard steps into the light to meet Jack

Jack (*handing over the empty mugs*) Another tea, please. For the lady.
Guard She's still here?
Jack Of course. Where would she go?
Guard Do you want another drink? (*He takes the mugs from Jack*)
Jack No. I'm coffee'd out.
Guard How is she?
Jack Oh, you know. A bit sad. We've been chatting.
Guard Look, don't take this the wrong way, but do you think perhaps she'd like to be left alone? (*He puts the mugs on to the coffee table*)
Jack I'm not bothering her. She obviously needs to talk.
Guard Well, don't be offended. But I might just pop along to make sure you're all right.
Jack Me? I'm fine.
Guard I'll just come along with you, sir.

SCENE 8

The railway carriage

A simple cross-fade from the L downlight to the benches and table brings the two characters into the new location

Guard Has she gone?
Jack She must have moved while I was with you.
Guard She's got six carriages to choose from not including First Class. They added a couple more just now. Didn't you feel the train being shunted?
Jack No, I didn't.
Guard Asleep?
Jack No. Not this time. (*Pause*) I'll have a look for her in a minute.

Guard There's no need.
Jack What do you mean?
Guard (*after an awkward pause*) Look, I'm pretty sure she got off the train.
Jack How could she? Shouldn't we call someone? What with the fog and everything?
Guard She was upset, wasn't she? Narrow face. Pretty, but narrow. And sort of ... well, I suppose the word for it is "haunted".
Jack That's right. So, you know her?
Guard Yes, I do. And we'd best leave her alone. It would be persecuting her to fetch the police and torches, and make a lot of fuss.
Jack "A lot of fuss." What are you talking about? Surely she needs to be found.
Guard We know about her. And when she turns up, we leave her to it, sort-of-thing.
Jack Has she escaped from somewhere?
Guard No, not strictly speaking. Not "escaped".
Jack What do you mean?
Guard It's late and the journey's boring. Are you sure you didn't just doze off? I mean, perhaps you dreamed her?
Jack But you've already made it clear you know who she is.
Guard I don't think so.
Jack Now you're being evasive.
Guard Perhaps you might have read something about this line?
Jack Definitely not. I told you, I'm not interested in railways.
Guard What was this lady wearing?
Jack She was dressed like something out of the nineteen-forties. It's a look that's coming back.
Guard There you are, then. I reckon you did read something. And you forgot about it. And now it's come back in your dream. Look!
Jack (*jumping out of his skin*) What!?!
Guard The fog has lifted. You can see the shunting yard. And the lights of the cars on the motorway. We'll be moving soon.

Scene 8

There is rumbling and clanking and the train starts to move off. A diesel engine this time – and the newer kind of continual track

Guard Ahh. There we are.
Jack You know who she is, then?
Guard We both do.
Jack Please. Can you just give me a straight answer?
Guard Why don't you just let it go? There are some things that just get pulled apart if you go on about them. It's kinder ... more civilized ... simply to leave a thing alone to get on by itself.
Jack Please don't go away. Let's sit down. I want you to tell me.
Guard (*sighing and sitting*) All right, then. But if I tell you, then you have to make me a promise.
Jack What is it?
Guard That you won't tell anyone else.
Jack All right, then.
Guard I hope you mean that, because I am going to hold you to it.
Jack Well, I don't understand how you could do that, but never mind — I promise.
Guard In nineteen forty-eight a woman jumped from the Fishguard to London night train as it went through Swindon.
Jack That's terrible.
Guard Indeed. And with nothing on her to say who she was.
Jack Did anyone claim the body?
Guard Oh, yes. Her husband. They lived somewhere in Sussex, of all places. He'd reported her missing. No one ever worked out why she'd done it. But people have secrets, don't they? And we ought to be tolerant of them, and not persecute folk simply for being human.
Jack I understand what you mean. But I don't see our woman jumping off a train. We talked, and she was much better after that. No, I don't think our passenger is going to kill herself.
Guard What if she already did?
Jack Pardon?
Guard Did you think she looked familiar? A bit like one of the old actresses?

Jack It definitely crossed my mind that I'd seen her before.
Guard I'm not going to say any more, I'm afraid. That's the modern world. Pick, pick, pick — until there's nothing left. This evening has been about you, not her. Remember her, and the things she said, and the way she held herself. Honour her in your memory. Learn from her. That's all she needs.
Jack What was her name?
Guard She was called Hope Cairns.
Jack "Hope". Sounds like that was in short supply, wouldn't you say?
Guard Yes. Poor thing.
Jack I'm glad I met her.
Guard Oh, yes?
Jack Actually I don't hate my wife, you know. I love her and I want ... her to love me back.
Guard Then make yourself loveable. Listen to Mrs Cairns.
Jack Blimey!
Guard What?
Jack You are every inch the sage, aren't you?
Guard Have I overdone it?
Jack No. You're a very good man for me to meet right now. Right man, right place, right time. Thank you.
Guard You're welcome. We do our best. Horlicks? You might still get a couple of hours sleep.
Jack Perfect. Yes, Dad — a mug of Horlicks would go down very well.
Guard Put your feet up and I'll bring it.

Jack settles himself on the L bench, looking wistfully at the place previously occupied by the Woman

Cross-fade to the blue scene change state. The image in the window changes as the moon fades out to leave a beautiful star-spangled clear night

Jack closes his eyes. The train rumbles on

Scene 9

The image in the window changes to the layered blue and pink of early sunrise, and then grows into a bright, yellow morning

The sound of the engine slowing, then coming to a gentle stop

SCENE 9

The same

The Lights fade up to a bright daytime state

The London Rail Steward (played by the same actor as the Stationmaster) enters briskly from R, *dressed in the garish uniform of a modern privatized rail carrier*

Steward Excuse me, sir.
Jack (*waking with a start*) What? Are we? Oh ...
Steward I'm afraid you'll have to leave the train.
Jack How did you get here?
Steward Pardon, sir?
Jack You were in Wales, just now.
Steward If only I were, sir. But I'm sorry to disappoint you as, in fact, I haven't been in Wales since two Christmases ago.
Jack You're not the stationmaster from Haverfordwest?
Steward Indeed not, sir.
Jack Is the guard still on board?
Steward I'm afraid not, sir. Is there a problem?
Jack I don't know. No. I just wanted to thank him.
Steward Come along now, sir. All the other passengers got off fifteen minutes ago.
Jack There weren't any other passengers. Well there was one other. But she left the train.
Steward You're a bit confused, sir. This was the Fishguard train that stopped at Haverfordwest, Swansea, Cardiff, Swindon and Reading. And there are always passengers.

Jack No. I got on a non-stopping train at twenty-five past eleven at Haverfordwest and there was only one passenger.
Steward Well, I don't mean to sound rude, but you're wrong. There hasn't been such a train for more than a decade. Now, please. I don't want to have to call a policeman.
Jack I was told to get on this train.
Steward "Told". Who by? Look, I'm sorry, I can't just stand here bandying words with the travelling public.
Jack What about the guard?
Steward I can't help you on that one.
Jack He made me tea and Horlicks.
Steward I can't imagine he did. Besides, what was the matter with the buffet?
Jack All right. I'm going.

The set brightens to a welcome, kind morning.

The London Rail Steward exits to L *while Jack struggles out of the booth and picks up his gear, then, dishevelled, walks to* DC *and addresses us directly*

SCENE 10

Paddington Station

Musak plays over the station PA and there are announcements. The concourse is thick with "the travelling public"

Jack So, there I was standing amidst the bustle of Paddington Station, feeling queasy and more than a little bit lost. People flowed around me, getting on with their business. I was hungry, and I had that feeling I used to get after an all-night party or an all-night retrospective at the NFT. Everything moving as if you're onboard a cross channel ferry in rough seas. (*He sighs*) Anyway. (*Pause*) Anyway, dream or not, I'm eternally

Scene 10

grateful to it, whatever it was, because the next thing I did was make a very important telephone call. Before setting out to place the drawings that I hoped would redeem me before my friend Tom in his Camden office, I called Harriet at home in Clapham. I asked her if she'd mind very much if I came home and stayed the night. I said ... right there, on the payphone at the station ... I said I thought perhaps she'd become friendly with someone else — someone who'd probably been kinder than I was, and I didn't mind. I asked her to have a think, and if she could bear it, then I'd prefer not to go back to Wales. I wanted to be with her. And the children. Because I love her. And them. (*Pause*) And what did she say? (*Pause*) She said "yes". And of all human conceits and strange inventions, I thanked heaven under my breath for the romance and the magic of the permanent way.

The sound of the concourse cross-fades into "Under Your Thumb"

Slow fade to black-out as Jack holds us in his emotional gaze

FURNITURE AND PROPERTY LIST

On stage: Two rows of bench seats
Table
Pile of expensive architectural journals and coffee table art books
Elegant "designer" coffee table. *On it*: trendy Mexican beer tray, half-empty bottle of Wild Turkey American bourbon whiskey, chunky glass tumbler, three American-style diner coffee mugs, nearly empty cafetiere, Claris Cliff teapot, matching milk jug, open packet of malted biscuits
Trendy Art Nouveau-style phone with a practical circular dialler
Upright Bauhaus-style armchair
Victorian piano stool
Heavy, old, expensive tweed jacket
Large, fashionable canvas satchel
Artist's portfolio

Off stage: Ancient bound railway timetable (**Guard**)

Personal: **Stationmaster**: whistle

LIGHTING PLOT

Practical fittings required: nil

To open: Semi-darkened stage with pools of "downlighter" light illuminating coffee table area DL and surface of table UC.

Cue 1	Music fades to the sound of a beach *Bring up vertical downlighter* CR	(Page 2)
Cue 2	**Tom**: "Put me out of my misery, will you?" *Fade downlighter* CR	(Page 3)
Cue 3	**Jack**: "... evenly on the station roof." *Cross-fade to blue wash*	(Page 5)
Cue 4	**Jack** and **Stationmaster** hunch against the weather *Cross-fade to night-time platform illuminated by powerful yellow sodium key light from* R	(Page 6)
Cue 5	**Stationmaster** exits *Cross-fade to blue wash*	(Page 8)
Cue 6	To open SCENE 3 *Cosy dappled pattern of ad-hoc illumination*	(Page 8)
Cue 7	**Jack** leans his head back *Cross-fade to blue wash*	(Page 12)
Cue 8	**Jack** searches behind the chair *Cross-fade to carriage lights in dappled pattern, as* SCENE 3	(Page 13)
Cue 9	**Woman**: "Thank you." *Cross-fade to blue wash*	(Page 14)

Cue 9	**Jack** walks downstage *Downlighter on coffee table* DL	(Page 14)
Cue 10	**Jack**: "Right — oh." *Short cross-fade to blue wash*	(Page 16)
Cue 11	**Jack** proffers the cups *Cross-fade to carriage lights*	(Page 17)
Cue 12	Lurching sound of carriages being coupled to a different engine *Cross-fade to blue wash*	(Page 22)
Cue 13	**Woman** walks resolutely off R *Cross-fade Lights to* L *downlight*	(Page 23)
Cue 14	**Guard**: "I'll just come along with you, sir." *Cross-fade to benches and table in carriage*	(Page 23)
Cue 15	**Jack** sits on the bench *Cross-fade to blue wash*	(Page 26)
Cue 16	To open SCENE 9 *Lights fade up to a bright daytime state*	(Page 27)
Cue 17	**Jack**: "All right. I'm going." *Lights brighten to a welcome, kind morning*	(Page 28)
Cue 18	"Under Your Thumb" plays *Fade Lights slowly to black-out*	(Page 29)

EFFECTS PLOT

Cue 1 To open　　　　　　　　　　　　　　　　　　(Page 1)
　　　　　"Under Your Thumb" by Godley and Creme plays

Cue 2 Lights come up on **Jack**　　　　　　　　　　(Page 1)
　　　　　Music fades to the sound of waves on a beach

Cue 3 **Jack**: "... evenly on the station roof."　　　　(Page 5)
　　　　　Subtle excerpt from "Under Your Thumb"

Cue 4 **Jack** and **Stationmaster** hunch against the weather　(Page 6)
　　　　　Music fades to steady, heavy rain

Cue 5 **Stationmaster** starts to walk away　　　　　(Page 7)
　　　　　Sound of train coming into the station

Cue 6 **Jack** collapses into the armchair　　　　　　(Page 8)
　　　　　"Under Your Thumb" plays

Cue 7 Lights come up for SCENE 3　　　　　　　　(Page 8)
　　　　　"Under Your Thumb" fades into the noise of a
　　　　　train travelling along modern, continuous tracks

Cue 8 **Jack**: "That's very kind."　　　　　　　　　(Page 9)
　　　　　Sound of continuous track fades to "clackety-clack"
　　　　　of old-fashioned segmented line

Cue 9 **Jack** leans his head back　　　　　　　　　(Page 12)
　　　　　Noise of train fades into "Under Your Thumb"

Cue 10 **Jack** searches behind the chair　　　　　　(Page 12)
　　　　　Cross-fade to sound of segmented tracks with chuffing
　　　　　of steam engine labouring up a long gradient

Cue 11	**Woman**: "Thank you." *Cross-fade to "Under Your Thumb"*	(Page 14)
Cue 12	**Jack** walks downstage to stand UL of the **Guard** *Cross-fade to sound of rails and steam engine*	(Page 14)
Cue 13	**Woman**: "There's so much I don't understand." *Train is losing momentum*	(Page 18)
Cue 14	**Jack**: "... stuck outside Swindon for a while." *Train stops with a slight jolt*	(Page 19)
Cue 15	**Jack**: "Don't go anywhere, will you?" *Sudden lurching sound of carriages being coupled to a different engine*	(Page 22)
Cue 16	**Guard**: "We'll be moving soon." *Rumbling and clanking and the train starts to move off, a diesel engine on the newer kind of continual track*	(Page 24)
Cue 17	Image in window changes to yellow morning *Sound of engine slowing, then coming to a gentle stop*	(Page 27)
Cue 18	To open SCENE 10 *Musak over station PA, announcements and sound of travelling public*	(Page 28)
Cue 19	**Jack**: "... and the magic of the permanent way." *Sounds of station fade into "Under Your Thumb"*	(Page 29)

PROJECTION PLOT

To open: Projected image of the moon visible in the top left corner of the window frame

Cue 1   **Jack**: "... somewhere, actually admires him."   (Page 4)
Image of moon slowly describes an arc from left to top right of frame

Cue 2   To open Scene 3   (Page 8)
Window projection of moon with clouds drifting across it

Cue 3   **Jack** sits on the bench   (Page 26)
Moon fades out to leave a star-spangled clear night

Cue 4   **Jack** closes his eyes. The train rumbles on   (Page 27)
Image changes to the layered blue and pink of early sunrise, and then grows into a bright, yellow morning

www.ingramcontent.com/pod-product-compliance
Lightning Source LLC
Chambersburg PA
CBHW070453050426
42450CB00012B/3260